TABLE OF CONTENTS

INTRODUCTION

Perhaps you have heard of 'Programming' and would really like to learn programming, but it seems very complicated. Terms like compiler, interface, instance, etc., don't sound right and may have made you take a step back.

It is also possible that your computer skills are very limited, perhaps surfing the Web, writing something in Word and not much else. You may not have a computer and use your mobile or tablet to manage online.

Now you have the opportunity to learn programming using this book and the Internet, since a web browser is enough to do your first jobs and get in touch with this exciting world. It is not necessary to install any development environment or special editor, not even a computer, you can use the device with which you connect to the Internet.

WHO SHOULD READ THIS BOOK

This book is aimed at those people who know absolutely nothing about programming or who have basic knowledge and want to learn about this discipline. It starts from scratch and progressively shows all the necessary knowledge with the aim of creating a solid and valid base for any programming language, although we will use Java.

HOW TO USE THIS BOOK

A programming book has to be, above all, practical. "You learn to program by programming." However, as they are readers who do not know this field, the theory is essential, but an attempt has been made to reduce it to the minimum necessary to adapt it to the corresponding level. The theory, more voluminous at the beginning, will give way to practice in each chapter, starting with the second and, as the book progresses, it will be reduced to its minimum expression.

We will need a programmable machine. One that can navigate is enough for us, that is, at least a smartphone or tablet and it is recommended to attach a keyboard via cable or bluetooth since when the lines of code begin to increase, the on-screen keyboard becomes quite tedious. An ordinary computer, tower or laptop type, without great features, connected to the Internet is, without a doubt, the ideal option.

All programs and code snippets have been checked by the author on the platform:

https://www.jdoodle.com/online-java-compiler/

with the Mozilla Firefox browser, version 110.0.1, under Windows 11.

GENERAL CONCEPTS

Chapter 1

1.1 Introduction

Before tackling programming itself, it is necessary to have an overview of the environment of programmable machines, some concepts related to them, the tools we will use and most importantly: how we will use them. We must learn well from scratch and rely on solid knowledge to understand everything that will come.

1.2 Some initial concepts

A machine concept could be:

"Aggregate of various parts ordered among themselves and directed to the formation of a whole."

On the other hand, if we are looking for a meaning of programming, we could say:

"Prepare certain machines or devices to start working at the time and in the desired way."

Concatenating both meanings we will have a more or less general idea of what a programmable machine is. We need a physical part, better known as **hardware**, which is invariable, and a non-tangible part, the program, also known as **software**, which varies according to the tasks we want our machine to perform. Both parts are necessary for our machine to be operational. Of course, hardware and software are only applicable concepts when we refer to a computer. And today any humble appliance, such as a refrigerator, already has one built into it. If we search for 'computer', it shows us:

"Electronic machine that, through certain programs, allows information to be stored and processed, and to solve problems of various kinds."

1.3 The hardware

A valid block diagram at this level could be the following:

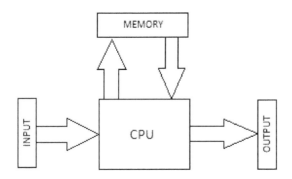

For a program to run, it must be loaded into main memory, represented here. This memory is volatile and its contents are lost when the computer is turned off. The CPU or Central Processing Unit is responsible for saving the program in memory first, to execute it later. Programs are generally stored permanently on the hard drive. In the input block, peripherals such as keyboard and mouse would be connected, while in the output block we could put a screen and printer, among others. Of course, everything is much more complex, but more information is not necessary at the moment.

1.4 The Software

When turning on the computer, the electronic circuits are powered and the BIOS (Basic Input Output System) of the Motherboard (motherboard) is awakened. On most computers it is possible to access its settings. The BIOS checks and configures the hardware and then passes control of it to the Operating System (OS).

"An operating system is a layer of software whose function is to manage all of the computer's hardware devices and to provide an appropriate interface for users and programs."

Perhaps, the complication in the previous concept comes from the word 'interface'. In Computer Science, an interface is an element that allows bidirectional communication. In the case that concerns us with the operating system, it corresponds to the environment that it creates on the screen so people can interact with the computer, while the actions of people will be converted to machine language, zeros and ones, which will understand the computer and vice versa, the actions of the hardware will be interpreted by the O.S. and show them to the user through the screen. This is the way the O.S. It acts as the interface between the user and the hardware.

The O.S. will also act as interface between hardware and programs, allowing them to be installed, deleted, authorizing access to resources, such as memory, peripherals, etc.

They are O.S. typical:

- Android and IOS, for tablets and smartphones.

- Linux, MacOS and Windows, for computers.

The programs, applications or app's are the software part dedicated to the user. Any app that comes to mind enters this classification, from an antivirus to an office suite, including a web browser or a file compressor.

1.5 Compilers and programming languages

We have left the concept of 'Programming' referring to a computer for last and among the many definitions, I always remember one that is not the most formal but the most expressive and reads like this:

"Programming is telling a fool very quickly exactly what he has to do at all times."

The very fast fool is the computer and the problem it has is precisely that. There is no reasoning ability (except for the latest A.I. projects) so we can only take advantage of its speed.

The fool, being a fool, only knows two states: '1' and '0', that is, he uses the binary system, although a variant of this called hexadecimal is usually used, which is more treatable when there are many digits. The data and instructions that the CPU handles must be in binary for it to be able to process them, it is what is known as **code or machine language**. The first computers that were built had to be programmed using this machine language. And it must be taken into account that each machine, depending on its hardware, has its own machine language different from the others. But machine language is horrible for people. A practical and efficient program written in machine language is a daunting and cumbersome task. To solve this problem, programming languages are born, closer to the language that humans use.

The execution of a program written using a programming language now has an extra stage, we have to convert our code in human language called **source code** into machine code. This operation is done by a program called the **compiler**. Our program, once compiled, can be executed as many times as we want.

THE JAVA LANGUAGE

Chapter 2

2.1 Some historical brushstrokes

In 1991, the Sun Microsystems company created, led by James Gosling, a programming language project for digital consumer devices. At first it was called Oak (oak) because this tree could be seen from the window of the team office, however, as it is a registered trademark they decided to change it to Java. Many theories speculate about the origin of this name, perhaps the most accepted has to do with his habit of drinking coffee.

Java fails in the field of digital devices at first, however, adapting well to Internet technology, they create their own HotJava browser, and in the year 1996, Java is supported by the great browser of the time: Netscape Navigator. .

Sun Microsystems was acquired by Oracle, well known for its Database Management System, in 2010, who has been in charge of Java ever since.

It is currently one of the most requested languages, as indicated by the TIOBE index.

The index can be used to check whether your programming skills are still up to date or to make a strategic decision about what programming language should be adopted when starting to build a new software system. The definition of the TIOBE index can be found here.

Mar 2023	Mar 2022	Change	Programming Language	Ratings	Change
1	1		Python	14.83%	+0.57%
2	2		C	14.73%	+1.67%
3	3		Java	13.56%	+2.37%
4	4		C++	13.29%	+4.64%
5	5		C#	7.17%	+1.25%
6	6		Visual Basic	4.75%	-1.01%

2.2 The philosophy of Java

It is based on five pillars.

Object oriented. It is a fully object-oriented language. Everything in Java is an object. This facet provides many advantages such as ease of management and software reuse.

Platform independence. The motto is "write it once, run it anywhere." In all operating systems it is possible to install a Java virtual machine (JVM), so that our program can be executed on all platforms.

Support for networking. So that a workgroup with its terminals connected to a network can work on the same project.

Code execution on remote systems. To allow client-server type applications, via network and Internet.

7

Easy to use. It takes the best of other languages such as C++, improving the syntax and eliminating complex structures such as pointers.

2.3 The Java compiler

Once our program has been written, it must be saved in a file that will have the extension **'.java'**, for example, helloWorld.java. The compiler will convert it to a '.class' file, helloWorld.class, which is called a **bytecode** file, which, unlike other programming languages, is not machine code, but intermediate code to be read by **the JVM interpreter** . At this level it does not affect us, but you should know that this is the case, because once the basics are learned, it is convenient to use an IDE (Integrated Development Environment) that facilitates the work of programmers when programs start to be more

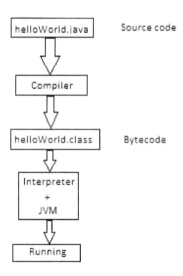

complex.

2.4 Our first program

```
public class HelloWorld {
        public static void main(String [] args) {
                System.out.println("Hello World.");
        }
}
```

To be a first program it has too many things, however, it is not possible to reduce it more. The order of reading and executing the statements of a program is from left to right and from top to bottom. We have already seen that Java is completely object oriented and precisely the first line already has the **class** keyword. A class is a template for creating an object, and all programs must have at least one. The 'public' keyword, which appears twice, is one of the possible access modifiers, which are also used by objects. Everything after the first brace and before the last brace belongs to the HelloWorld class, that is, our first integer program.

The second line contains a **method** or **procedure**. It is used to group related performances that must be executed in the same batch, successively. However, this is a very special procedure, it is the **main** procedure, there can only be one, and it is the first one that is executed in any Java program. Procedures can accept **arguments** and would be enclosed in parentheses after the main keyword. In this case, as it is the main method, you always have to put the following instruction:

(String [] args)

which corresponds to an **array** of type String (chain of characters) called args. We will see all these concepts throughout the book. Presenting this first program forces us to show many elements whose meaning we will not understand until after a few chapters, but we should not worry since everything will work out.

We are left with a sentence that is the only one that contains our main method between its braces. Let's note that it ends in a semicolon, which is how all statements should end.

System.out.println("Hello World.");

This statement is actually calling the println() method that prints the argument that we pass between the parentheses on the screen. The **dot operator** (.) also appears, indicating that println() belongs to the output stream **out**, which in turn belongs to the **System** class.

We can install an IDE (Integrated Development Environment) like NetBeans or Eclipse on our computer to compile and run this program and all the ones that we will make. However, at this level, if we do not want complications it is better to use an online compiler. There are tons of them on the Internet. I have chosen JDoodle as I could have chosen any other. This is the link:

https://www.jdoodle.com/online-java-compiler/

Once JDoodle is open in the browser, we will write the code as we have it on the previous page. It is very easy to make a mistake at the beginning, a comma instead of a semicolon, a few single quotes instead of double quotes and the thousand and one mistakes that we will make without realizing it when transcribing. Once our code is written we will press the execute button and if everything has gone well, we will see on the

Result screen what our program is expected to do. If we have not written it correctly, instead, we will get a series of error messages that will give us some clue as to where we have gone wrong.

The web page itself offers us more options, by pressing the ellipsis button, including saving the source file on our computer with the save (to local file) option. You can also save online, but registration is required.

2.5 Exercises

It is imperative that you check all your exercises in the compiler.

1. Modify our program so that it displays your full name.

2. Idem above to get the following result with the same order:

My name is:

Name Surname

and I live in mycity.

3. Let's try, without explanation, the concatenation operator (+) and let's mix two different data types. On the screen should appear your age written in number, which we will have previously programmed inside println().

I am myage.

You will need to use the concatenation operator twice.

CONSTANTS AND VARIABLES

Chapter 3

3.1 Some theory

In order to create programs that are considered adequate and useful, it is necessary to achieve certain objectives. Talking about the objectives of the programs that we will carry out in this introductory book does not make much sense, but it does make sense when we work in the professional field and even more so when a program is created by several programmers where Software Engineering techniques are applied. .

Three, are the basic objectives of programming.

1. Correction. A program must deliver adequate results and not produce erroneous effects such as exceptions, remain memory resident after being closed, etc.

2. Clarity. It is necessary to use comments that adequately explain the darker parts of the program to be able to maintain it by ourselves or by other programmers, as well as to have a clear and orderly style when writing the source code.

3. Efficiency. A program will be considered more efficient the fewer resources it consumes. If in the treatment of a database, for example, an application occupies 90% of the memory capacity, it will not be considered efficient.

All these objectives must be taken into account when programming and we will improve as our knowledge increases.

3.2 The primitive data types of Java

Everything in Java is an object... except the primitive data types. Perhaps we should start by defining what data is:

"A data is information about something concrete that allows its exact knowledge."

Depending on what we want to assess, the data must have an appropriate nature, that is, if we are talking about age, it must be numerical and if a logical expression is to be evaluated, it will be true or false. These differences force us to define different types of data, which in Java are called primitives, to distinguish them from objects and there are specifically eight types, four of the integer type, two of the decimal type, one of the true/false type and another of the character type. , that is, letters, numbers and symbols.

We will work with these four types:

int which means integer. These are non-decimal numbers, both positive and negative.

float from floating point. for decimal numbers. It is represented with an 'f', upper or lower case, at the end.

char from character. It includes letters, numbers and symbols. They must be enclosed by single quotes.

boolean That it can only take the value of true or false. They are used to evaluate logical (Boolean) expressions.

In this link, belonging to the Java API, all the primitive types are explained:

https://docs.oracle.com/javase/tutorial/java/nutsandbolts/datatypes.html

3.3 The concept of variable

When talking about a variable, the mathematical concept that we have all learned quickly comes to mind: "element of the function that takes values." It is a variable because its value changes.

In computing, a variable is a location in memory that stores a value.

Variables in programming are used to store values, the bigger the object, the more memory it will occupy. Three operations are performed on the variables.

Statement. It must be given a name and a data type. It must end in a semicolon.

int age;

Initialization. That is, give an initial value. The memory area where the variable is set usually contains residual bits from other old elements and it can causes exceptions.

age = 35;

Assignment. It is the value change operation, once the variable is already working. It has the same syntax as initialization. Notice that the assignment operator is the symbol '='.

Declaration and initialization can coincide in the same statement:

int age = 35;

3.4 Constants

It could be said that a constant is a variable that does not change its value. It must be declared and initialized at the same time. The assignment operation will always give us an error, as expected. In Java, constants are declared according to the following statement:

static final float PI = 3.141592F;

As a mnemonic rule, a constant is declared and initialized by adding the words static and final to the declaration of a variable.

3.5 A more useful program

Let us calculate the length of a circle of given radius.

```java
public class LengthC{
        static final float PI = 2.141592F;
        public static void main (String [] args){
                float L = 0F;
                int radio = 5;
                L = 2 * PI * radio;
                System.out.println("L = " + L + " cm.");
        }
}
```

The formula to calculate the length of a circle is:

$$L = 2 \cdot PI \cdot radius$$

When dealing with decimal numbers we must use the primitive data type 'float', remember that it is a numeric expression with a decimal point that must end with the letter 'f' or 'F', although depending on the compiler, it could be dispensed with.

Java is a strongly typed language and that means that when we relate data, all of it must be of the same type. Since there is a float, PI, in the formula, the result, L, must also be of type float. If we have doubts, it is best to put all the data in float, including the literal 2 that would pass to 2F and the radius that would be written as:

float radius = 5F;

although the program would be less efficient since we are spending more memory than necessary for the same purpose, because the float type needs more bytes than the integer type.

We have also used the product operator (*) in the formula and the concatenation operator (+), which we already knew, to obtain the results on the screen using the println() method.

Write and compile the code. Then change all the data in the formula to float and compile again. Test the code by modifying those things that you have doubts about. Practicing is how you really learn to program.

3.6 Exercises

It is imperative that you check all your exercises in the compiler.

1. Write a program that calculates the area of a square with side 5 cm.

2. Modify the previous program so that it calculates the area of a rectangle with base 5 cm and height 7 cm.

3. Modify problem number 2 again and using its data, calculate the area of the triangle. (A = b x h/2).

4. Write a program that calculates the perimeter of the **equilateral** triangle in the previous problem.

5. Write a program that calculates the area of a 5 cm circle. radio. (Area of the circle = PI x radius^2 = PI x radius x radius).

ELEMENTS OF A PROGRAM

Chapter 4

In the previous chapter we introduced constants and variables. Each one of them must have different names in our programs, which in programming are called **identifiers**. In addition, we must also know which operators we can apply to our types of data.

And let's not forget one of the most important programming goals discussed in Chapter 3, **clarity**, which is enhanced by the use of **comments**.

4.1 Identifiers

Continuing with the clarity, the identifiers are usually composed of words that define the variable or component in question and four variants are usually used by convention to differentiate these words.

UpperCamelCase: the name of Camel is due to the similarity with the sinuous silhouette of the camel, when we combine upper and lower case letters. This type proposes that all the words that make up the identifier go with the first letter in uppercase. It is recommended in **class and interface** identifiers. For example:

class HelloWorldInEnglish

lowerCamelCase: Similar to the previous one, but the initial of the first word is lowercase. It is often used in **variables** and **methods**.

int VehicleInitialColor

lowercase: all lowercase. It is recommended in **packages**. A package contains a set of classes.

geometricdrawingpackage

SCREAMING_SNAKE_CASE: where the words are all uppercase and separated by underscores. Snake means that the identifiers resemble the shape of a snake when written in all capital letters. It is used in constants.

static final float NUMBER_OF_EULER

Although we already know how to use upper and lower case in our identifiers, we still have to know its writing rules:

- Valid characters are the English alphabet (a-Z), digits (0-9), underscore, and dollar($).

- The first character cannot be a digit.

- Each identifier must have at least one character.

- Reserved words cannot be used.

The keywords come from the English vocabulary. We can see them all in the link:

https://docs.oracle.com/javase/tutorial/java/nutsandbolts/_keywords.html

Interestingly, true, false and null are not there because they are considered literals.

4.2 Some initial operators

Operators represent those operations that can be performed on the data. Some are similar to the mathematical ones, others are logical and there are also comparison ones. We will present them as we need them. In this section we will see which we learn in school.

Addition / concatenation. The symbol '+' is used. It is also used to concatenate character strings as we have already practiced in previous exercises.

"My name is:" + "John Smith"

Subtraction. The symbol '-' is used.

Product. The symbol used is the asterisk '*'.

Division. Use the slash '/' as a symbol. The drawback of division comes when using integer (int) data. If the division is not exact, the result is rounded to the nearest lower integer:

$$7 / 2 = 3$$

so if an exact result is needed in our program, we must resort to the float type.

Module or remainder of the division. Its symbol is the percentage '%'. It is only valid for the int type and the other integer types. Gets the remainder of the division.

$$7\% \; 2 = 1$$

This operator is widely used to obtain even numbers, prime numbers, etc.

4.3 Comments

As we have already anticipated, comments represent a very important element of clarity, giving meaning to code fragments that either take a long time to locate, or their complex operation requires an explanation to future programmers who must maintain the program.

Comments can be **multi-line**, in which case, they start with '/*' and end with '*/'.

/* Program that calculates the length of a circle, giving as data the constant PI, of the float type, and the radius of the circle, of the int type, according to the formula L = 2 x PI x radius. */

One line comments. They start with two slashes '//'. They can be in the snippet header or on the side and are then called margin comments.

//Formula for the length of the circumference.

L = 2 * PI * radius // radius is of type int.

CONTROL STRUCTURES

Chapter 5

Control structures provide programs with decision capabilities and extra computational capabilities. They are components of Structured Programming.

Assimilation of this chapter is a giant step, since we would already have all the necessary tools to deal with any algorithm that we need to implement.

5.1 Structured programming

Structured programming states that any program can be written using only three basic types of control structures.

1. Sequence. Instructions are read and executed from left to right and from top to bottom.

2. Selection. The evaluation of the logical expressions will indicate which is the next instruction to be executed.

3. Iteration. A calculation strategy consists of repeating a set of instructions until a condition is true and the jump to another instruction in the main sequence is allowed.

Therefore, if a problem can be solved, that is, an algorithm can be extracted, we can implement it with the three options of structured programming. However, in programs with many lines of code, structured programming is not enough and we must also use **Modular Programming**, which we will see later in the book.

5.2 Relational and logical operators

When selection and iteration structures are being executed, it is necessary to compare values or solve logical expressions and the result of this will always be true or false, which will indicate to our structures where they should follow.

Relational operators.

Equal. Its symbol is '=='. It's a typical mistake putting '='.

Less / Less than or equal. '<' / '<='.

Greater / Greater or equal. '>' / '>='.

Distinct. '!='. For example, 5 != 5 evaluates to false.

Logical operators.

&& is known as logical AND. Both terms must be true for it to evaluate to true.

|| It is a logical OR. It is enough for a term to be true for it to evaluate to true.

Some examples.

(5 > 3) && (3 == 3) --> true

(7 >= 7) && (3 != 3) --> false, for the second term

(7 >= 7) || (3 != 3) --> true, because it is enough for one term to evaluate to true

(3 >= 5) || (9 <= 4) --> false, both terms are false.

5.3 Selection structures

5.3.1 if, if – else, else if

The selection structure par excellence is the 'if' conditional, providing decision-making capacity:

"If there is bread left, buy 2 loaves"

This 'if' can go alone or accompanied by an 'else' that it would look like this:

"If there is bread left, buy 2 loaves"

"and if not, buy donuts."

The entire structure can be nested increasing the complexity as many times as necessary for our program. When more than one line of code follows these instructions, it is necessary to enclose it in braces. Let's see some examples.

Code snippet that finds out if a number is even.

if (number % 2 == 0) System.out.println("the number: " + number + "is even");

else System.out.println("The number: " + number + " is odd");

Apart from the operation of the if – else clauses, in this snippet we can see how the module operator is used. If the remainder of division by 2 is zero, the number is even. We can also see the equality operator '==' and the '+' operator working as a concatenation of three elements, two of the String type, which we will see later, and one of the int type.

Code snippet that converts a numeric mark to textual in Spanish schools.

```
if ( grade == 0 || grade == 1 || grade == 2) System.out.println(" Very poor");

else if (grade == 3 || grade == 4) System.out.println("Insufficient");

else if(grade == 5) System.out.println("Enough");

else if(grade == 6) System.out.println("Good");

else if(grade == 7 || score == 8) System.out.println("Notable");

else if(grade == 9) System.out.println("Outstanding");

else if (grade == 10 ){

        System.out.println("HONORS");

        System.out.println("Decorated by the Director");
}
```

In this fragment you can see, in the first line, the use of the OR operator, whose symbol is '||', when the grade is 0 or 1 or 2, the logical expression is evaluated to true and the grade is printed on the screen . Note that we can include as many if-else-if statements as we need. And if there is more than one statement, as is the case with the last else if, they must be enclosed in braces.

However, the structure of this code snippet is functional but not elegant or overly clear. Therefore, it is convenient to use the **switch** structure that we will see in the next section.

5.3.2 switch

Many of the solutions adopted with the structures of the previous section can be made with a switch in a more elegant way and improving clarity. However, not all data types are valid, we can only use String, int and char. It has the following form:

switch(variable) {

        case value1:   instructions; **break**;

        case value2:   instructions; **break**;

        ....

        default: instructions; **break**;

}

If a variable value is not covered by the case statements, then the **default** statement will handle it. The **break** at the end is used to get out of the switch and it may not be interesting to put it in all cases, although it is normal. It all depends on the programmer. On the other hand, it is possible to group several values in a single case, separated by commas.

If we convert the fragment of the previous qualifications, as a switch block, it will be:

```
switch ( grade ) {

    case 0, 1, 2: System.out.println("Very poor"); break;

    case 3, 4: System.out.println("Insufficient"); break;

    case 5: System.out.println("Enough"); break;

    case 6: System.out.println("Good"); break;

    case 7, 8: System.out.println("Notable"); break;

    case 9: System.out.println("Outstanding"); break;

    Case 10:

        {

                System.out.println("HONORS");
                System.out.println("Decorated by the Director");
                break;

        }

    default: System.out.println("Not evaluated"); break;

}
```

5.4 Iteration structures

The idea of iteration structures is to repeat a block of code, several times, until a certain value is reached, at which point the loop ends.

5.4.1 The for loop

It is, without a doubt, the most popular loop in programming. It consists of an initialize, a finalize, and an increment separated by semicolons. The letters i, j, and k are often used for variables. The next loop makes exactly 10 turns before exiting.

for (int i = 1; i < 11; i ++) System.out.println("Lap: " + i);

The conditions are at the discretion of the programmer. We would also have gotten 10 iterations with the following:

for (int i = 0; i < 10; i++)

Or with these others:

for (int i = 10; i > 0; i--)

As the reader can see, we have used a new operator without previous explanation, it is the **increment/decrement** operator. It is also very popular. Equals:

i = i + 1 or i = i − 1

The value of the variable i is added or subtracted by 1 and the result is saved again in the variable itself, replacing the one that was there.

5.4.2 while, do-while

As long as the condition is met, the loop will be executed. It is possible to implement a for loop using while, but not always the other way around, because the while loop is more versatile. The loop of 10 iterations would look like this:

```
int i = 1;

while ( i < 11 ) {

        System.out.println ( "Lap " + i );

        i++;

}
```

We also have the do-while structure. In this case the first iteration is always performed, since loop control is at the end.

```
int i = 1;

do {

        System.out.println ( "Lap " + i );

        i++;

} while (i < 11);
```

5.5 Command line arguments

Before the arrival of operating systems with beautiful and intuitive user interfaces through icons and windows on computers, screens were completely black and the only interaction with the operating system was through text commands. That interface is still alive today, in Windows for example, it is called Command Prompt, in other operating systems, simply Terminal.

When writing a command in the terminal, if the program allows it, we can put the arguments or parameters that we want it to take and in this way the user decides what arguments they will be.

This is the way we will simulate user input into our programs from now on. In JDoodle there is a field called **CommandLine Arguments** that is used for this purpose where the data will be separated by blank spaces.

Our program will collect the data through the arguments of the main method, that is, the String array called **args** that all Java programs carry:

main(String[] args)

To rescue the first argument we will use the index 0, that is, args[0], for the second args[1] and so on. But if we have written 3 pieces of data on the command line and request a fourth, through args[3], we will get a nice exception:

java.lang.ArrayIndexOutOfBoundsException

which indicates that we have gone outside the array bounds.

Let's do a quick test program.

```
public class CommandLine{

    public static void main(String [] args){

        System.out.println("The data entered is: " +
            args[0] + " " + args[1] + " " + args[2]);

    }

}
```

Write this program in JDoodle. Introduce in CommanLine Arguments, three names or three numbers separated by blank spaces and then using the execute button, check that our program reads them.

There is an obstacle if we want to work with the int type on the command line. The data stored in args is of String type. When we need them to be of type int to use them with mathematical operators, we have to do a conversion. We use the **parseInt()** method of the **Integer** class, which is a wrapper class for the int type that transforms a String into an int.

```
int number = Integer.parseInt( args[0] );
```

Later we will study arrays and methods. You will then understand in depth these instructions that you are handling now by an act of faith.

5.6 Exercises

It is imperative that you check all your exercises in the compiler. Respect the order because they are exercises of progressive difficulty.

1. Complete the first fragment of section 5.3.1 to print on the screen, if the number entered by command line is even or not.

2. Idem above for the second fragment.

3. Idem above for the fragment of section 5.3.2

4. Repeat exercise 1, but in this case, tell us if it is a multiple of three.

5. Idem above that prints on the screen, separated by commas, all the numbers in increasing order up to the number given by means of a for structure. Use **print()** to avoid the line break.

6. Same as above, but only print even numbers up to the given number, using a while structure.

7. "FIZZ BUZZ". Write a program that implements this well-known algorithm, which prints on the screen, in ascending order, the numbers from 1 to 100, separated by commas, but if the number to be printed is a multiple of 3, FIZZ is printed instead. If the number is a multiple of 5, BUZZ is printed. And if it is a multiple of 3 and 5 at the same time, FIZZBUZZ is printed.

8. Adjust the previous exercise so that there is a line break every 15 numbers. It then finishes off the presentation by matching the columns by commas, numbers, and words. It isn't difficult.

METHODS

Chapter 6

The previous chapter gives us the keys to implement any algorithm. However, if as the size of the programs increases, you want to improve their efficiency or the complexity of the algorithm is very high, we must resort to **modularity**, which is achieved through methods, classes and packages. A class can have multiple methods and a package multiple classes. The structuring in classes and packages, more generically known as Object Oriented Programming, should be the next objective of the reader.

6.1 Advantages

If a program repeats the same lines of code several times, a method, also known as a function or procedure, should be created to group them together, thus reducing the size of the program. In the same way, if within a program there are well differentiated parts, it could be interesting to also group them into methods. Grouping the code will always improve the clarity of the programs and will help the programmer to focus on the specific aspects to be solved, gaining in efficiency.

That said, of course you can program without methods, and in our exercises we didn't need them, but by structuring our programs with methods, everything becomes easier or at least clearer.

.

6.2 Definition

We already have an example of how a method is defined in our first program and in all the ones we have done, since we have always needed the **main** method.

public static void main (String [] args) {

--> INSTRUCTIONS <--

}

- **Access modifier**: public, protected, private. These reserved words indicate which elements have access to the method. They only make sense when working with classes.

-**static**. Tells the compiler that this method will be kept in memory until the program exits.

- **Type of return**. Indicates the type of data that the method will return. To do this, the **return** keyword is used. In our main method we do not return anything and therefore this word is not there, which implies that we must put **void** in the return data type.

- **Method name**. In our case it is **main**. Remember that it is advisable to use the lowerCamelCase system when naming our methods.

- **Arguments**. It is the natural way of accessing data. They must be in parentheses and separated by commas. Each argument must have its data type and then its name, in which lowerCamelCase still advises. In this case it is an array of Strings called **args**, which curiously is short for arguments referring to the command line.

- **Start and close braces {}** All instructions in the procedure must be between these two braces.

6.3 Call or invocation

A procedure is called or invoked by its name and the name of its arguments. For example, if we have this method written somewhere in the program:

void goodMorning(String dayTime){

    if (dayTime == "day") System.out.println("Good morning");

    else System.outprintln("Good night");

}

The call would be:

goodMorning(dayTime);

When the call refers to a method of another class, we must use the **dot operator** (.) next to the class name.

    System.out.println(" ");

    Integer.parseInt (args[0]);

The Java compiler requires us that within the main class, the one that contains the main method, that is, all of our programs, <u>all methods must be static.</u>

6.4 Example program

In this example, the procedure will calculate the maximum of two numbers entered per command line.

```
public class Maximum {

    public static void main ( String[] args) {

        int number1 = Integer.parseInt ( args[0] );

        int number2 = Integer.parseInt ( args[1] );

        int max = getMaximum ( number1, number2 );

        System.out.println("The maximum is: " + max );

    }

    static int getMaximum ( int num1, int num2){

        if (num1 > num2) return num1;

        return num2;

    }

}
```

Notice how the only variables that the procedure can use are the ones it receives as parameters, **num1 and num2**. The **return** clause is duplicated to return, wherever called, the maximum of the two numbers. For this reason we have dumped it into a variable, **max**, although it would also have been possible to embed it directly inside println(). We must clearly distinguish the difference between the definition, where all the instructions of the method are programmed, and its invocation.

6.5 Exercises

1. Write a program that uses two procedures, Exercise 5.6.1 and Exercise 5.6.4.

2. Write a program that receives a date (dd mm yyyy) with a method that checks if it is correct, ie it is not greater than 31 days and not greater than 12 months. You must write the date on the screen or say that it is incorrect. Use the boolean type as the return of the function.

3. Write a program that prints on the screen how many digits the entered number has. You must have a method that returns an int with the number of digits. The algorithm is obtained by counting successive divisions by 10 until zero.

4. Write a program that prints on the screen all the divisors of a number given by the command line. You must have a procedure that, when asked if a number is a divisor of another, responds with a boolean type.

ARRAYS

Chapter 7

Arrays or vectors are groups of data of the same type, very helpful in certain cases. We'll see them in this chapter, along with the String type, which is a very special type in Java. Let's not forget that every program we've ever made has an array of Strings in the main method.

7.1 Building an array

The declaration of an array does not differ much from the rest of the elements, if we add the pair of square brackets:

boolean [] state;

int [] speed;

float [] [] coords;

String [] args;

The first two declarations are one-dimensional vectors and the last two are two-dimensional. They can have as many dimensions as we need, "if we are able to handle them". Initialization is very specific since arrays are objects and require the **new** clause:

state = new boolean [10];

speed = new int [25];

coords = new float [10] [15];

We must not work with an uninitialized array. We can also use explicit initialization, if we know the initial data.

char [] vowel = {'a', 'e', 'i', 'o', 'u'};

boolean [] state = {false, true, false};

Remember that access to the array is done by indicating the position of the element and that the first position is always position **zero**. According to the above statements:

vowel[0] --> 'a'

state[2] --> false

vowel[5] --> "IndexOutOfBoundsException"

The last access attempt throws an exception because index 5 does not exist and we have gone out of bounds.

7.2 Operations

7.2.1 Traversal

The traversal is one of the fundamental operations on a vector, supporting other tasks such as searching, printing or ordering.

An array, as the object that it is, has a series of methods and attributes (class variables) that will help us in its manipulation. One of the more useful attributes is **length**, which will give us an int of its length. Also use the dot operator (.) Using the vowels vector from the previous section:

int limit = vowel.length;

Our variable limit will have a value of 5

For loops fit nicely with vector traversal. Let's see an example with the vowel array.

for (int i = 0; i < vowel.length; i ++) {}

If we wanted a screen print, we could use **print()**:

for (int i = 0; i < vowel.length; i ++) {

    System.out.print(vowel[i] + ", ");

}

For search, that is, finding the position of a certain element would be:

int position =-1;

char item = 'u';

for (int i = 0; i < vowel.length; i ++) {

    if (vowel[i] == item) position = i;

}

if (position == -1)

    System.out.println("Item not found");

7.2.2 java.util.Arrays

This class provides several methods that assist the programmer in common tasks with vectors.

The comparison may seem obvious but it is not. If we use the equality operator '==', we are really checking if it is the same object, which does not solve anything for us. To check if two vectors have the same elements and in the same order, use the equals() method.

java.util.Arrays.equals(vowel, state) --> false

A direct way to print a vector on the screen would be:

System.out.println(java.util.Arrays.toString(vowel));

And if we wanted an ordering:

java.util.Arrays.sort(numbers);

7.2.3 Use of vectors in methods.

An array is a data type that can be passed as an argument to a method and can also be returned by a **return** clause. The implementation of a method that returns a vector and accepts another two as arguments, would be:

static int[] myMethod (int[] num1, int[] num2){ statements }

And the call:

myMethod(num1, num2);

7.3 The String class

Working directly with the char type can be complicated in most cases. For this reason Java has the String class, which might seem like a primitive type for some operations, like assignment, but it isn't. It is literally an array of characters that we treat as a single piece of data.

Initialization is done like any primitive type. Once initialized, a String object is immutable, that is, it is not possible to modify any of the characters that compose it, it can only be given a new value.

String name = "Peter";

The addition operator (+) is used on strings as a concatenator

"solo" + "mil" + "lo" --> "solomillo"

There are many methods of manipulation. You can see them all here:

https://docs.oracle.com/javase/7/docs/api/java/lang/String.html

Let's explain a few. Based on the previous String name we have:

Comparison. Use the equals() method.

name.equals("peter"); --> false

Length of a String. Note that in this case it takes parentheses unlike the length of an array.

name.length(); --> 6

Access to individual characters. The first char has the index zero.

name.charAt(1);--> 'e'

Conversion from int to String.

String numberWord = String.valueOf(number);

String to int conversion

int number = Integer.parseInt(numberString);

If numericString has any non-numeric characters, the compiler will throw a **NumberFormatException**. The last two operations are due to the fact that the compiler does not see these two instructions as the same type, since, obviously, they are not, but they use the same number symbols:

int year = 2023;

String year = "2023";

7.4 Exercises

1.Write a program that creates an array of 5 integers and stores the five numbers given by the command line. You must implement a method to save the values, another to take their arithmetic mean, and a third to display everything on the screen.

2. Write a program that creates a String of a famous phrase or reasoning written on the command line and then displays it on the screen.

3. Create two arrays of 5 positions, saving the names of five students in one, and in the other, under the same index, the corresponding grades. The program must search for the student and modify his mark according to the values entered by the command line.It must indicate if cannot find the student.

4. Write a palindrome checker for a number entered by command line. A number is a palindrome if it reads the same both ways, for example, 3207023.

EPILOGUE

Chapter 8

My dear reader, here ends the introduction to programming that I thought it convenient for you to assimilate. I hope you have had a proper progression, that you have not been bored and that you have reached the level you expected.

There have been many things that I did not want to include so as not to increase this volume, and not to saturate you too much.

These would be the reinforcement points in which you should continue your learning.

- **The import clause**, to be able to use already written classes, which will help us in our programming tasks.

- **Terminal input Stream**, for keyboard data entry at any time. We have always used command line input.

- **The Math class**, which will help us with more advanced mathematical operations, trigonometry, powers, roots and random numbers that are to fill in, for example, our vectors or emulate lottery-style games.

- **Object Oriented Programming** should be your next goal. In Java everything except primitive types are objects. If you have assimilated the theory and have done all the exercises, you already have a good base to start with, or in any other similar one such as Python, C++, or C#.

.

.

8.1 Final challenges.

1. Program that prints all prime numbers up to the upper bound given by the command line. It requires a double control loop.

2. Program that draws a rhombus of at's with a horizontal diagonal value given by the command line. For the values 1, 2 and 3 it would be:

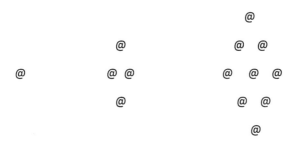

3. Own implementation of a sorting algorithm. When you enter a set of unordered values, separated by spaces, on the command line, the program should print the ordered vector on the screen. For the implementation, the first element is considered ordered and a traversal is made from the element to be ordered, exchanging values or not as appropriate. It requires a double control loop.

SOLUTIONS

Chapter 2

1. See exercise 2.

2.

```
public class MyName {

        public static void main(String [] args) {

                System.out.println("My name is:");

                System.out.println("Peter Smith");

                System.out.println("and I live in London");

        }

}
```

3.

```
public class MyAge {

        public static void main(String [] args) {

                //Attention to spaces so as not to join words

                System.out.println("I am " + 23 + " years old");

        }

}
```

Chapter 3

1.
```
public class Square {
        public static void main(String [] args) {
                int area = 5 * 5;
                System.out.println("Area = " + area);
        }
}
```

2.
```
public class Rectangle {
        public static void main(String [] args) {
                int area = 7 * 5;
                System.out.println("Area = " + area);
        }
}
```

3.
```
public class Triangle {
        public static void main(String [] args) {
        // The denominator must be float to avoid integer division
                float area = (7 * 5)/2F;
                System.out.println("Area = " + area);
        }
}
```

```
4. public class PerTriangle {
        public static void main(String [] args) {
                int perimeter = 5 + 5 + 5;
                System.out.println("Perimeter = " + perimeter);
        }
}
5. public class CircleArea {
        static final float PI = 3.141592F;
        public static void main(String [] args) {
                float area = PI * 5 * 5
                System.out.println("Area = " + area);
        }
}
```

.

Chapter 5

1. See exercise 3.

2. See exercise 3.

3. public class Ratings{

    public static void main(String [] args){

      int note = Integer.parseInt(args[0]);

     switch (note) {

        case 0, 1, 2: System.out.println("Very poor"); break;

        case 3, 4: System.out.println("Insufficient"); break;

        case 5: System.out.println("Enough"); break;

        case 6: System.out.println("Good"); break;

        case 7, 8: System.out.println("Notable"); break;

        case 9: System.out.println("Outstanding"); break;

        case 10: {

            System.out.println("HONORS");
            System.out.println("Decorated by the Director"); break;
            }

        default: System.out.println("Not evaluated"); break;

     }

    }

}

4. See exercise 3.

5., 6. and 7. See exercise 8.

8. public class FizzBuzz {

```
public static void main(String args[]) {
    for(int i = 1; i<=100; i++){
        if((i % 3 == 0) && (i % 5 == 0)){
            System.out.print("FIZZBUZZ, ");
        }
        else if (i % 3 == 0) System.out.print("FIZZ, ");
        else if (i % 5 == 0) System.out.print("BUZZ, ");
        else {
            //Adjust columns
            if (i < 10) System.out.print(" " + i + ", ");
            else System.out.print(i + ", ");
        }
        //So that there is a row every 15 numbers
        if (i % 15 == 0) System.out.println();
    }
}
}
```

Chapter 6

```java
1. public class parityThree {
       public static void main(String args[]) {
               int number = Integer.parseInt(args[0]);
               divTwo(number);
               divThree(number);
       }
       static void divTwo(int num){
               if (num % 2 == 0)
                       System.out.println(num + " is even.");
               else System.out.println(num + " is not even.");
       }
       static void divThree(int num){
           if (num % 3 == 0)
               System.out.println(num + " is a multiple of three.");
               else System.out.println(num + " is not a multiple of
                                                three.");
     }
}
```

```
2. public class Date {

        public static void main(String args[]) {

                int day = Integer.parseInt(args[0]);

                int month = Integer.parseInt(args[1]);

                int year = Integer.parseInt(args[2]);

                boolean isOk = checkDate(day, month, year);

                //It is not necessary to put (isOk == true)

                if(isOk) System.out.println(day + "/" + month + "/" +
                                                            year);

                else System.out.println("Wrong input.");

        }

        static boolean checkDate(int day, int month, int year){

                if( (day <32) && (month <13) ) return true;

                else return false;

        }

}
```

```
3. public class Digits {
    public static void main(String args[]) {
        int number = Integer.parseInt(args[0]);
        int numDigits = digNumber(number);
        System.out.println("The number " + number + " has " + numDigits
                                            + " digits.");
    }

    static int digNumber(int num){
        int counter = 0;
        while (num > 0){
            num = num/10;
            counter++;
        }
        return counter;
    }
}
```

```java
4. public class Divisors {
        public static void main(String args[]) {
                int number = Integer.parseInt(args[0]);
                System.out.print("The divisors of " + number + " are: ");
                for ( int i = 1; i<=number; i++){
                        if(isDivisor(number,i)) System.out.print(i + ", ");
                }
        }
        static boolean isDivisor(int num, int index){
                if(num % index == 0) return true;
                else return false;
        }
}
```

Chapter 7

```
1. public class ArrayMedia {

        public static void main(String args[]) {

                int[] numbers = new int[5];

                save(args, numbers);

                float meanA = getAverage(numbers);

                printing(numbers,meanA);

        }


        static void save(String[] args, int[] numbers){

                for (int i = 0; i<5; i++){

                        numbers[i] = Integer.parseInt(args[i]);

                }

        }


        static float getAverage(int [] numbers){

                int sum = 0;

                for (int i = 0; i<5; i++){

                        sum = sum + numbers[i];

                }
```

```java
            return(sum/5F);
    }


    static void printing(int [] numbers, float meanA){
            System.out.print("The vector " +
                    java.util.Arrays.toString(numbers));

            System.out.print(" has mean: " + meanA);
    }
}
2. public class Phrases {
    public static void main(String args[]) {
            String phrase="";
            for(int i = 0; i<args.length; i++){
                    phrase = phrase + " " + args[i];
            }
            System.out.println(phrase);
    }
}
```

```
3. public class Students {
    public static void main(String args[]) {
        String [] students = {"John", "Peter", "Francis", "Rose", "Sara"};
        int[] notes = {7, 6, 5, 8, 4};
        System.out.print(java.util.Arrays.toString(students));
        System.out.println(java.util.Arrays.toString(notes));
        boolean found = false;
        for(int i = 0; i<students.length; i++){
            if(students[i].equals(args[0])){
                notes[i]= Integer.parseInt(args[1]);
                found = true;
            }
        }
        if(!found) System.out.println("Student not found");
        System.out.print(java.util.Arrays.toString(students));
        System.out.println(java.util.Arrays.toString(notes));
    }
}
```

```java
4. public class Palindrome{
        public static void main(String [] args){
                int length = args.length;
                int [] numbers = new int[length];
                int [] reverse = new int[length];
                for(int i = 0; i<args.length; i++){
                        numbers[i]=Integer.parseInt(args[i]);
                        reverse[(length-1)-i] =Integer.parseInt(args[i]);
                }
                if(java.util.Arrays.equals(numbers,reverse))
                        System.out.println("It's palindrome");
                else System.out.println("Not palindrome");
        }
}
```

Chapter 8

1. *public class Primes{*

    public static void main(String [] args){

        int limit = Integer.parseInt(args[0]);

        boolean prime;

        System.out.print("1, ");

        for(int i = 2; i<=limit; i++){

            prime = true;

            for(int j = 2; j<i; j++){

                if(i % j == 0) prime = false;

            }

            if(prime) System.out.print(i + ", ");

        }

    }

}

2. It prints line by line from top to bottom. Each line has whitespace at first and then a sequence of one or more at signs + space. It can be calculated exactly according to the line in which we are, how many elements of each are needed. The rhombus is divided into two halves, from the beginning to the horizontal diagonal in one loop and what remains below, in another loop.

```
public class RhombAt {

    public static void main(String args[]) {

        int length = Integer.parseInt(args[0]);

        // Loop of upper lines
        for(int i = 1; i<=length; i++){

            //Left spaces
            for(int j = 1; j<= (length -i); j++){

                System.out.print(" ");

            }

            //at signs + spaces
            for(int k = 1; k<=i; k++){

                System.out.print("@ ");//a space

            }

            System.out.println();

        }
```

```
            //Loop bottom lines
        for(int ii = length - 1; ii>0; ii--){
                //Left spaces
            for(int jj = 1; jj <= length -ii; jj++){
                System.out.print(" ");
        }
            //at signs + spaces
            for(int kk = ii; kk>0; kk--){
                System.out.print("@ ");
        }
            System.out.println();
    }
    }
}
```

3. The length method is used, applied to the vector args. The first for loop stores the input data in the numbers array. The first element is considered ordered. Each element is compared with the entire vector, if an element is greater an exchange is made, calling the method interCambiar(). This algorithm is not the most efficient, but it meets the difficulty level of this book.

```java
public class Sort {
    public static void main(String args[]) {
        int [] numbers = new int[args.length];
        //Save input data
        for(int i = 0; i<args.length; i++){
            numbers[i] = Integer.parseInt(args[i]);
        }
        System.out.println(java.util.Arrays.toString(numbers));
        //Sort algorithm
        for(int i = 1; i<numbers.length; i++){
            for(int j = 0; j<numbers.length; j++){
                if(numbers[j]>numbers[i])
                    swap(i,j,numbers);
            }
        }
        //end vector
        System.out.println(java.util.Arrays.toString(numbers));
    }
    static void swap(int i, int j, int[] numbers){
        int temp = numbers[i];
        numbers[i] = numbers[j];
```

```
                numbers[j] = temp;
        }
}
```